Weekly Reader Books presents
Using Your Head

A Children's Book about Effective Thinking and Learning

by

Joy Wilt

Illustrated by Ernie Hergenroeder

Educational Products Division
Word, Incorporated
Waco, Texas

Author

JOY WILT is creator and director of Children's Ministries, an organization that provides resources "for people who care about children"—speakers, workshops, demonstrations, consulting services, and training institutes. A certified elementary school teacher, administrator, and early childhood specialist, Joy is also consultant to and professor in the master's degree program in children's ministries for Fuller Theological Seminary. Joy is a graduate of LaVerne College, LaVerne, California (B.A. in Biological Science), and Pacific Oaks College, Pasadena, California (M.A. in Human Development). She is author of three books, *Happily Ever After, An Uncomplicated Guide to Becoming a Superparent,* and *Taming the Big Bad Wolves,* as well as the popular *Can-Make-And-Do Books.* Joy's commitment "never to forget what it feels like to be a child" permeates the many innovative programs she has developed and her work as lecturer, consultant, writer, and—not least—mother of two children, Christopher and Lisa.

Artist

ERNIE HERGENROEDER is founder and owner of Hergie & Associates (a visual communications studio and advertising agency). With the establishment of this company in 1975, "Hergie" and his wife, Faith, settled in San Jose with their four children, Lynn, Kathy, Stephen, and Beth. Active in community and church affairs, Hergie is involved in presenting creative workshops for teachers, ministers, and others who wish to understand the techniques of communicating visually. He also lectures in high schools to encourage young artists toward a career in commercial art. Hergie serves as a consultant to organizations such as the Police Athletic League (PAL), Girl Scouts, and religious and secular corporations. His ultimate goal is to touch the hearts of kids (8 to 80) all over the world—visually!

This book is a presentation of Weekly Reader Books.
Weekly Reader Books offers book clubs for children from
preschool through junior high school.

For further information write to:
WEEKLY READER BOOKS
1250 Fairwood Ave.
Columbus, Ohio 43216

Using Your Head

ISBN: 0-8499-8134-4
Library of Congress Catalog Card Number: 79-50071
Bruce Johnson, Editor

5 / 84 83

Contents

Introduction

Using Your Head is one of a series of books. The complete set is called *Ready-Set-Grow!*

Using Your Head deals with effective thinking and learning, and can be used by itself or as a part of a program that utilizes all of the *Ready-Set-Grow!* books.

Using Your Head is specifically designed so that children can either read the book themselves or have it read to them. This can be done at home, church, or school. When reading to children, it is not necessary to complete the book at one sitting. Concern should be given to the attention span of the individual child and his or her comprehension of the subject matter.

Using Your Head is designed to involve the child in the concepts that are being taught. This is done by simply and carefully explaining each concept and then asking questions that invite a response from the child. It is hoped that by answering the questions, the child will personalize the concept and, thus, integrate it into his or her thinking.

Using Your Head teaches that everyone is born with a desire and a need to think and learn. Our minds are constantly working, even when we are asleep—whether we are aware of our thoughts or not. We do not do anything without thinking about it first.

Because children need and want to learn, they are curious about things. And curiosity doesn't kill cats—nor does it kill children. In fact, curiosity motivates children to learn.

Using Your Head is designed to help children explore things they are curious about safely and intelligently.

Children need to be encouraged to learn on their own about things that interest them, so that they can develop learning skills and a feeling of competence.

Using Your Head

If you would like to learn more than you know now

this book is for you.

Every person has a desire to...

think and know things.

Most people think more than they realize. A person thinks . . .

CHECKERS

all day long . . .

and all night long.

In fact, a person does not do anything without thinking first.

14

Thinking comes before doing.

Every action requires thinking of some kind. **15**

Some thinking happens without our being aware of it.

This kind of thinking takes place when we walk, eat, and talk. When we do these things, we hardly notice that we are thinking at all.

Other thinking requires concentration and hard work.

This kind of thinking takes place when we solve problems, study, and read. We know we are thinking when we do these things because they always take a lot of effort to do.

Discovering and learning things takes the kind of thinking that requires concentration and hard work.

Most people, no matter who they are or how old they are, already know a lot.

But no one knows everything there is to know.

You know a lot. In fact, you probably know more than you think you do. To prove this is true, see if you can answer the questions on the following pages.

How many
of these animals can you name?

Can you count from one to one hundred?

Can you say the entire alphabet?

What does this sign mean?

What do the colors on this traffic signal mean?

Can you name these shapes?

Here are some holiday symbols.

Do you know what holiday each one stands for?

31

Do you know where these foods come from?

Well, how did you do with those questions? You probably did pretty well.

You may even have thought that the questions were very easy. If you did, that was only because you already knew the answers.

It is true that you already know a lot, but you do not know everything there is to know. You can learn a lot more than you know now. This book is going to tell you how.

Chapter 1

Curiosity

Every person wonders about things.

Every person wants to know about things.

Wondering and wanting to know about things is called curiosity.

When a person wonders or wants to know about something, he or she could be called curious.

39

There is an old saying that says . . .

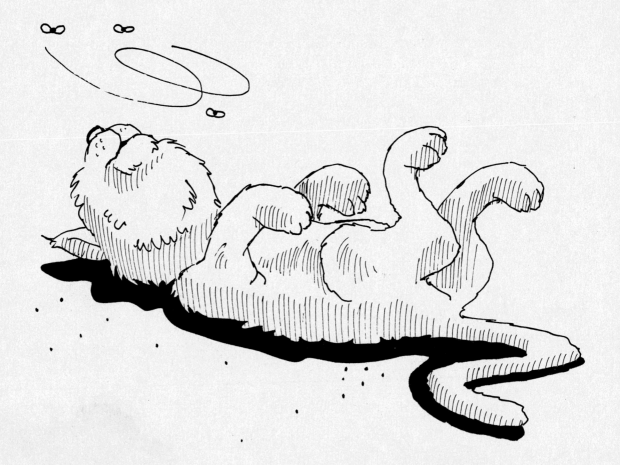

"Curiosity killed the cat."

But this is not true!

Curiosity doesn't kill cats, and neither does it kill people. In fact . . .

Every person is born with curiosity.

Curiosity is the desire that makes people want to learn and know things.

What are you curious about?

What do you wonder?

What would you like to know about?

Have you ever been curious about yourself?
Do you ever wonder . . .

     where you came from,

     why you are the way you are,

     how your mind and body work,

     what will happen to you after you die?

Have you ever been curious about where other things come from?
Have you ever wondered . . .

"Where do dust and dirt come from?"

"Where does air come from?"

Have you ever been curious about why things are the way they are?
Have you ever wondered . . .

"Why are people all different colors, shapes, and sizes?"

"Why do animals look and act the way they do?"

49

Have you ever been curious about how things work?
Have you ever wondered . . .

"How do these things work?"

Have you ever been curious about what happens to things?
Have you ever wondered . . .

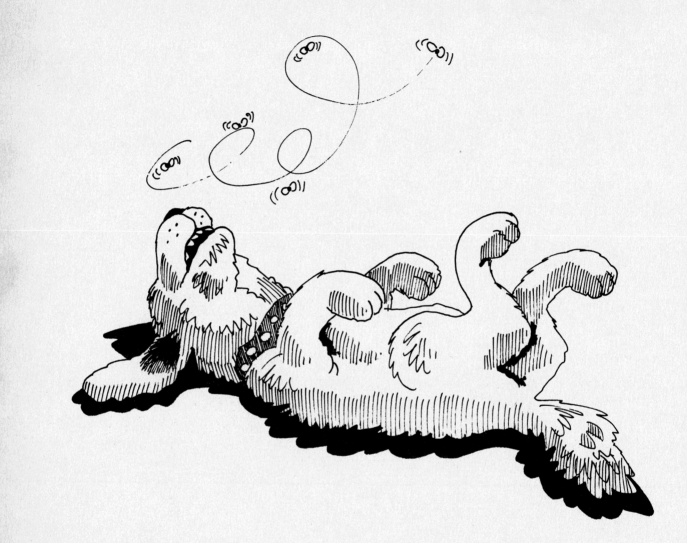

"Where do animals go after they die?"

"What happens to a plant after it dies?"

What are some things you are curious about? In the space below,
list the things you wonder about.

_____

_____

Where do things come from?

_____

_____

Why are things the way they are?

_____

_____

How do things work?

_____

_____

What happens to things?

_____

_____

It is good for you to wonder about things.

Curiosity is very important. But it is only the beginning to learning and knowing things.

Once you realize you are curious about something, it is time for you to find out about it. The next chapter is going to tell you how to find out about things.

Chapter 2

Exploration

It is possible for every person to find out about the things he or she is curious about.
How?

By exploring.

Exploring means that you try to find out about something by investigating it.

You study and examine it carefully.

There are many ways to explore something.
One way to explore something is to <u>observe</u> it.

When you observe something, you . . .

look at it closely or
watch it carefully.

Another way to explore something is to <u>experience it</u>.

When you experience something, you . . .

feel it, listen to it, taste it (if it is something you can eat), try it, or smell it. **65**

Another way to explore something is to ask <u>questions</u> about it.

When you ask questions about something, be sure to ask someone who can and will give you the right answers.

67

Another way to explore something is to <u>read</u> about it.

You can read books, magazines, and newspapers in order to explore something.

These can be bought, or they can be borrowed from your school or community library.

Another way to explore something is to <u>experiment</u> with it.

When you experiment with something, you work with it. You try it out and test it.

There are at least five different ways to explore something.

You can . . .

    observe it,
    experience it,
    ask questions about it,
    read about it, or
    experiment with it.

You can do all of these things yourself. To prove that this is true, do the activities on the following pages. Have fun while you are exploring!

OBSERVING

Find a spider or an insect of some kind. Observe it for at least fifteen minutes and see what you can learn about it by watching.

Do the same thing with a dog, cat, bird, machine, appliance, or anything else you might choose to observe.

The next time your mom or dad goes shopping, go along and pick an out-of-the-way spot in the store where you can do some observing. Look around from your spot as long as your parent is shopping. What can you learn by watching?

APPLES
59¢ Lb.

CABBAGE
19¢ Lb.

POTATOES
8¢ Lb.

SPECIAL
CARROTS
15¢ Lb.

Do the same thing at a gas station, post office, school, library, church, or anywhere else you can observe.

The next time you watch television, watch one program and make a list of the things you learned while watching it.

Next time you go to the show, make a list of the things you learned while watching the movie.

EXPERIENCING

Take a pan outside and fill it with water. Experience the
water. Try to hold some in your hands. Can you? Pour
some on the ground. What happens to it? What does
water look like? What does it taste like? Does it have
a smell? What sounds can water make?

Do the same thing with mud, Play-doh, flour, sand,
corn starch mixed with water, or anything else you
can experience.

Take a walk outside. List at least ten sounds, sights, or smells that you never noticed before.

While you are walking, take a small bag with you and collect things you find along the way. Take the objects you find home with you and experience them. Look at them, feel them, listen to any sounds they make or that can be made with them, smell them, and if it is safe, taste them.

ASKING QUESTIONS

See how many of these riddles you can solve by asking questions. Ask people you think will give you the right answers.

Riddle #1: A boy's grandfather is only six years older than the boy's father. How can this be true?

Riddle #2: Two sisters who were born on the same day to the same parents and who looked alike said they were not twins. Why?

Riddle #3: If a plane carrying US citizens crashed on the border between Mexico and the United States, where would the survivors be buried?

Riddle #4: An archeologist found two gold coins dated 39 BC. He knew at once they were fakes. How?

Riddle #5: A man went for a walk. It started to rain. He didn't have a hat or an umbrella. His clothes and shoes got wet, but his hair didn't get wet. Why?

Riddle #6: Two men played checkers. They played three games, and each man won two. How?

Riddle #7: A boy went to the dentist to get a cavity filled. The boy was the dentist's son, but the dentist was not the boy's father. Why?

Riddle #8: A woman unwrapped a cube of sugar. She put it into her coffee, but the sugar didn't get wet. Why?

Answers to these riddles are on page 121.

READING

See if you can answer these two questions by reading books, magazines, or newspapers from your home, school, or library.

What happens to food after you eat it?

Why are there seeds inside most fruits? 83

EXPERIMENTING

Put five tiny pieces of paper in the palm of your hand. See if you can blow the pieces of paper off your hand . . .

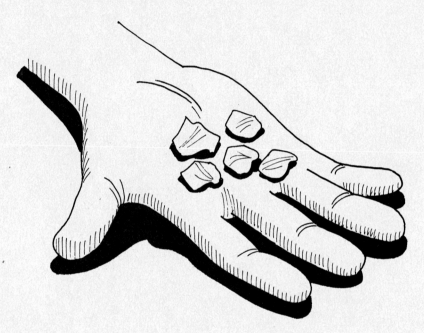

but only blow off one piece at a time.

Answer to this problem is on page 122.

Get a one-dollar bill and a quarter. Without using anything else, balance the quarter . . .

on the edge of the dollar bill.

Answer to this problem is on page 123.

Stand on a bathroom scale. How much do you weigh?
Guess what would happen if you lifted one foot off the scale.
How much do you think the scale would show you weigh?
Try it and see if your guess was right.

Guess what would happen if you stood on two bathroom scales at the same time placing one foot on each scale. What do you think each scale would read? Try it and see if your guess was right.

Can you place a sheet of newspaper on the floor in such a way that when two people stand face to face on the paper they won't be able to touch each other?

You are not allowed to cut or tear the newspaper. Neither can you tie up the people in any way to keep them from moving. *Answer to this problem is on page 124.*

Can you make four triangles that all have the
same length sides with six toothpicks?

Place fifteen toothpicks in the positions shown
below. Can you take away six toothpicks and
leave ten?

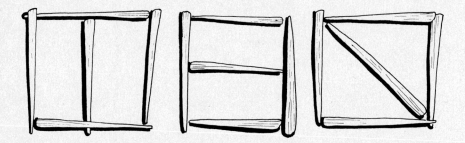

Place five toothpicks in a row on the table as shown
below. Can you add six toothpicks to the five and
make nine?

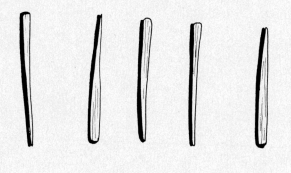

Can you use toothpicks to show that half of eleven
is six?

Answers to these problems are on page 125.

Place twenty-four toothpicks in the positions shown below to form nine squares. Can you take away only eight toothpicks and leave only two squares?

Answer to this problem is on page 126.

Can you cut a two inch by four inch piece of paper into a loop which you could step inside of and pass up over your entire body? Try it. You can't use any glue or tape. Cut one solid loop without any breaks in it.

90

Answer to this problem is on page 127.

Take a piece of rope about two feet long. Grab one
end of the rope with your right hand. Hold the other
end of the rope with your left hand.

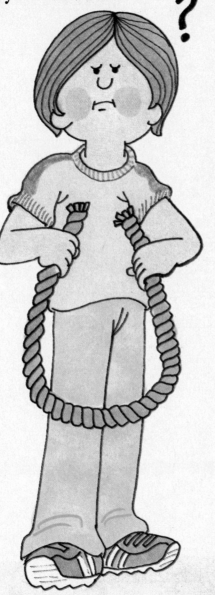

Try to tie a knot in the rope without letting go
of the ends which are held in each hand.
Answer to this problem is on page 128.

Whether you explore by observing, experiencing, asking questions, reading, or experimenting, exploring is fun. But just as exciting is knowing things and being able to remember them. That is what the next chapter is all about.

Chapter 3

Knowing and Remembering

Once you have been curious about something and explored it, you usually know about it.

can be fun.

Knowing about something . . .

can help you at school.

96

Knowing about something can help you at home.

Knowing about something can help you when you are playing.

I'D BETTER PULL THE ROOTS OUT IF I DON'T WANT THESE WEEDS TO GROW BACK.

Knowing about something can help you when you are working.

Knowing things is very important.

But remembering things is just as important.

Remembering means bringing something you already know from the past into your mind.

OH, I KNOW! I REMEMBER WHERE I LEFT MY SHOES. THEY ARE IN THE LIVING ROOM BY THE TV.

Remembering helps you put the things you already know into use. 103

Remembering is very important because knowing something won't help you if you can't remember it.

Almost every person has an ability to remember.

This way everyone can think of things from the past.

You can remember things.

You can remember what things look like. To prove this is true, get a sheet of paper and do this activity.

Try to remember what these objects look like and then draw a picture of each one.

Tree

Chair

Flower

Ball

Worm

Cloud

You can remember what things smell like. To prove this is true, look through this list of things that you have probably smelled before. Try to remember whether or not you liked the smell of each item in the list.

Rose

Dead animal (for example: a skunk, a fish, or a mouse)

Vomit

Onion

New pair of shoes

Fresh loaf of bread

You can remember what things taste like. To prove this is true, look at each thing on this page and try to remember if it tasted sweet, sour, spicy hot, or salty.

You can remember what things sound like. To prove this is true, remember what these things sound like and try to make a similar sound.

Dog barking
Cat meowing
Telephone ringing
Person humming "Jingle Bells"
Electric mixer
Clock

You can remember what things feel like. To prove this is true, look at each thing on this page and try to remember if it feels rough, smooth, cold, or hot.

You can remember people that you have met, seen on TV, or read about.

Try to remember these people.

Who was your first teacher?
Who was your first friend or playmate?
Who is president of the United States?
Who is your favorite famous person?

You can remember experiences that you have had.

Try to remember these events.

> What happened on your last birthday?
> What happened the last time you visited the doctor or dentist?
> What was the best thing that ever happened to you?
> What was the worst thing that ever happened to you?

You can remember ideas or information that you have learned.

Try to remember some of these things you probably know.

What is your home address or phone number?
What is the capital of the state you live in?
How many days are there in the month of September?
How many dimes does it take to make five dollars?

Conclusion

You already know a lot, but you do not know everything there is to know.

You have a curiosity that makes you want to learn and know things.

By exploring you can find out about the things you want to learn and know about. There are many ways to explore something.

You can . . .

      observe it,

      experience it,

      ask questions about it,

      read about it, or

      experiment with it.

Once you have learned something, it becomes a part of everything you know. It becomes something for you to remember and use as you grow and become the marvelous person you are meant to be!

Now <u>that's</u> really . . .

Using your head!

ANSWERS

If you want to check your answers to the riddles on pages 80 and 81, here are the correct answers.

Riddle # 1: The grandfather is the father of the boy's mother.

Riddle # 2: The two sisters were born in different years.

Riddle # 3: The survivors would not be buried at all.

Riddle # 4: BC means before Christ was born. At the time when the coins were supposedly made, no one knew exactly when Christ was going to be born in order to place 39 BC on the coins. In addition, the modern system of dating the years AD and BC was not begun until 500 to 600 years after the dates on the coins.

Riddle # 5: The man was bald.

Riddle # 6. They weren't playing against each other. They were playing other partners.

Riddle # 7: The dentist was the boy's mother.

Riddle # 8: The woman put the cube of sugar into a jar of instant coffee.

A good solution to the problem on page 84 is to hold four pieces of paper with your other hand while you blow one piece off. Then hold three pieces and blow again.

Do this until you have blown off all the pieces of paper on your hand one at a time.

Here is a good solution to the problem on page 85.

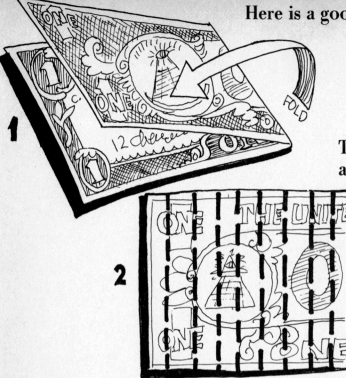

Take a one-dollar bill and fold it in half as shown in figure one.

Fold the dollar bill about eight times to make it look like a folded paper fan as shown in figure two.

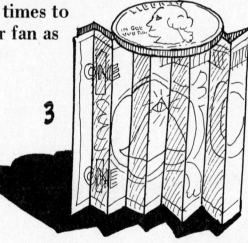

Place the folded dollar bill on a table and balance the quarter on the top edge of the bill as shown in figure three.

NEWSPAPER

A good solution to the problem on page 87 is to place the newspaper on the floor in a doorway, have two people step on the edge of the paper, facing each other, and then close the door. They are both standing face to face, and yet they can't touch each other.

Here are good solutions to the problems on page 88.

These six toothpicks make four triangles that all have the same length sides.

Fifteen toothpicks . . . take away six toothpicks . . . leaves . . .

Five toothpicks . . . add six toothpicks . . . makes . . .

Half of eleven is six? Form the Roman numeral eleven with three toothpicks as shown. Cover the bottom half of the Roman numeral eleven with your hand or a piece of paper to make the Roman numeral six.

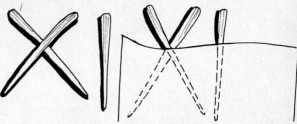

Here is a good solution to the problem on page 89.

Here is a good solution to the problem on page 90.

Take a two inch by four inch piece of paper and cut down the center of the paper as shown in figure one.

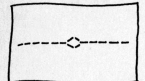

1.

2.

3.

Fold the piece of paper along this cut and make a series of cuts as shown in figure two above. All cuts should be about one-eighth inch apart and should stop about one-quarter of an inch from the edges or center.

HEY, IT WORKS!

Stretch the paper out to make a large loop or ring as shown in figure three above. Place the loop on the floor, step inside it, and slip the loop up over your head. Try it!

1.
2.
3.

I DID IT!

4.

Here is a good solution to the problem on page 91. Lay the rope out in a straight line. Then cross your arms as shown in figure one. Now pick up one end of the rope in each hand as shown in figure two. Now uncross your arms while continuing to hold on to the ends of the rope. As you unfold your arms, you will find that the rope will tie a knot in itself automatically. See figures three and four.